GOD'S PROMISES

on His Love

CONTENTS

for

_____

from

_____

I am sure that nothing now, nothing in the future, no powers, nothing above us or nothing below us—nothing in the whole created world—will ever be able to separate us from God's love that is in Christ Jesus our Lord.

—Romans 8:38–39 (ERV)

Biblica Publishing
We welcome your questions and comments.

USA   1820 Jet Stream Drive, Colorado Springs, CO 80921
           www.Biblica.com

God's Promises on His Love
ISBN 978-1-934068-97-7

Livingstone project staff includes Andy Culbertson, Linda Taylor,
Joan Guest, Everett O'Bryan. Interior design by Lindsay Galvin and
Larry Taylor.

Published in 2008 by Authentic.

A catalog record for this book is available from the Library of Congress.

Printed in the United States of America

God Calls Us to Love

IS LOVE

And so we know and rely on the love God has for us. God is love. Whoever lives in love lives in God, and God in him.

—1 John 4:16 (NIV)

This is real love—not that we loved God, but that he loved us and sent his Son as a sacrifice to take away our sins.
—_1 John 4:10 (NLT)_

Then Christ will make his home in your hearts as you trust in him. Your roots will grow down into God's love and keep you strong. And may you have the power to understand, as all God's people should, how wide, how long, how high, and how deep his love is. May you experience the love of Christ, though it is too great to understand fully. Then you will be made complete with all the fullness of life and power that comes from God.
—_Ephesians 3:17–19 (NLT)_

But the Lord has always loved his followers. And he will continue to love his followers forever and ever! God will be good to their children and to their children's children.

—*Psalm 103:17 (ERV)*

Long ago the LORD said to Israel: "I have loved you, my people, with an everlasting love. With unfailing love I have drawn you to myself."

—*Jeremiah 31:3 (NLT)*

This is how God showed his love among us: He sent his one and only Son into the world that we might live through him.

—*1 John 4:9 (NIV)*

There is no fear in love; but perfect love casts out fear, because fear involves torment. But he who fears has not been made perfect in love.

—*1 John 4:18 (NKJV)*

Lord, your true love is higher than the sky. Your loyalty is higher than the clouds.

—*Psalm 36:5 (ERV)*

"For the mountains shall depart and the hills be removed, but My kindness shall not depart from you, nor shall My covenant of peace be removed," says the LORD, who has mercy on you.

—*Isaiah 54:10 (NKJV)*

Show me your unfailing love in wonderful ways. By your mighty power you rescue those who seek refuge from their enemies.

—*Psalm 17:7 (NLT)*

But Christ died for us while we were still sinners. In that way God showed us that he loves us very much.

—*Romans 5:8 (ERV)*

We love Him because He first loved us.

—*1 John 4:19 (NKJV)*

Give thanks to the God of heaven. His love endures forever.

—*Psalm 136:26 (NIV)*

Your unfailing love is better than life itself; how I praise you! I will praise you as long as I live, lifting up my hands to you in prayer.

—*Psalm 63:3–4 (NLT)*

But because of his great love for us, God, who is rich in mercy, made us alive with Christ even when we were dead in transgressions—it is by grace you have been saved.

—*Ephesians 2:4–5 (NIV)*

See how very much our Father loves us, for he calls us his children, and that is what we are! But the people who belong to this world don't recognize that we are God's children because they don't know him.

—*1 John 3:1 (NLT)*

For as the heavens are high above the earth, so great is His mercy toward those who fear Him.

—*Psalm 103:11 (NKJV)*

And so we know and rely on the love God has for us. God is love. Whoever lives in love lives in God, and God in him.

—*1 John 4:16 (NIV)*

The Lord's love and kindness never ends. His compassion never ends. Every morning he shows it in new ways! Lord, you are so very true and loyal! I say to myself, "The Lord is my God, and I trust him."

—*Lamentations 3:22–24 (ERV)*

The Lord is happy with people who worship him. The Lord is pleased with people who trust in his true love.

—*Psalm 147:11 (ERV)*

For God loved the world so much that he gave his one and only Son, so that everyone who believes in him will not perish but have eternal life.

—*John 3:16 (NLT)*

Love is patient and kind. Love is not jealous or boastful or proud or rude. It does not demand its own way. It is not irritable, and it keeps no record of being wronged. It does not rejoice about injustice but rejoices whenever the truth wins out. Love never gives up, never loses faith, is always hopeful, and endures through every circumstance. Prophecy and speaking in unknown languages and special knowledge will become useless. But love will last forever!

—*1 Corinthians 13:4–8 (NLT)*

God's Love IS COMPASSIONATE

They refused to listen. They forgot the
amazing things you did with them!
They became stubborn. They decided
to return to Egypt and became slaves
again! But you are a forgiving God!
You are kind and full of mercy. You are
patient and full of love. So you didn't
leave them!
       —*Nehemiah 9:17 (ERV)*

The LORD is gracious and righteous;
our God is full of compassion.
       —*Psalm 116:5 (NIV)*

I will betroth you to Me forever; yes, I
will betroth you to Me in righteousness
and justice, in lovingkindness and
mercy.
       —*Hosea 2:19 (NKJV)*

The Lord is good to every person. God shows his mercy to everything he made.
—*Psalm 145:9 (ERV)*

So the LORD must wait for you to come to him so he can show you his love and compassion. For the LORD is a faithful God. Blessed are those who wait for his help.
—*Isaiah 30:18 (NLT)*

The eyes of the LORD are on the righteous and his ears are attentive to their cry.
—*Psalm 34:15 (NIV)*

We say that those people who accepted their troubles with patience are now happy. You have heard about Job's patience. You know that after all Job's trouble, the Lord helped him. This shows that the Lord is full of mercy and is kind.
—*James 5:11 (ERV)*

Blessed be the God and Father of our Lord Jesus Christ, the Father of mercies and God of all comfort.

—*2 Corinthians 1:3 (NKJV)*

In my distress I called to the LORD; I cried to my God for help. From his temple he heard my voice; my cry came before him, into his ears. . . . He reached down from on high and took hold of me; he drew me out of deep waters. He rescued me from my powerful enemy, from my foes, who were too strong for me.

—*Psalm 18:6, 16–17 (NIV)*

I led them with cords of human kindness, with ties of love; I lifted the yoke from their neck and bent down to feed them.

—*Hosea 11:4 (NIV)*

LORD, how great is your mercy; let me be revived by following your regulations.
—*Psalm 119:156 (NLT)*

"For the mountains shall depart and the hills be removed, but My kindness shall not depart from you, nor shall My covenant of peace be removed," says the LORD, who has mercy on you.
—*Isaiah 54:10 (NKJV)*

Then, as soon as our ancestors were rested, they started doing terrible things again! So you let the enemy defeat them and punish them. They called to you for help, and in heaven you heard them and helped them. You are so kind! That happened so many times!
—*Nehemiah 9:28 (ERV)*

Let your compassion come to me that I may live, for your law is my delight.
—*Psalm 119:77 (NIV)*

God's Love IS KIND

But God, who is rich in mercy,
because of His great love with which He
loved us, even when we were dead in
trespasses, made us alive together with
Christ (by grace you have been saved),
and raised us up together, and made
us sit together in the heavenly places in
Christ Jesus.

> —*Ephesians 2:4–6 (NKJV)*

Remember to be kind to me, Lord.
Show me the tender love that you have
always had. Don't remember the sins
and bad things that I did when I was
young. For your good name, Lord,
remember me with love.

> —*Psalm 25:6–7 (ERV)*

Keep yourselves in the love of God,
looking for the mercy of our Lord Jesus
Christ unto eternal life.
—Jude 1:21 (NKJV)

The LORD is close to the brokenhearted;
he rescues those whose spirits are
crushed.
—Psalm 34:18 (NLT)

God, look at me and be kind to me. Do
what is right for the people who love
your name.
—Psalm 119:132 (ERV)

Be merciful to me, O God, be merciful
to me! For my soul trusts in You; and
in the shadow of Your wings I will make
my refuge, until these calamities have
passed by.
—Psalm 57:1 (NKJV)

Who is a God like you, who pardons sin and forgives the transgression of the remnant of his inheritance? You do not stay angry forever but delight to show mercy.

—Micah 7:18 (NIV)

So let us come boldly to the throne of our gracious God. There we will receive his mercy, and we will find grace to help us when we need it most.

—Hebrews 4:16 (NLT)

And David said to Gad, "I am in great distress. Please let me fall into the hand of the LORD, for His mercies are very great; but do not let me fall into the hand of man."

—1 Chronicles 21:13 (NKJV)

He shows mercy from generation to generation to all who fear him.

—Luke 1:50 (NLT)

Praise be to the God and Father of our Lord Jesus Christ. God has great mercy, and because of his mercy he gave us a new life. This new life brings us a living hope through Jesus Christ's rising from death.

—*1 Peter 1:3 (ERV)*

I will be glad and rejoice in your love, for you saw my affliction and knew the anguish of my soul.

—*Psalm 31:7 (NIV)*

God, be merciful to me, because of your great loving kindness, because of your great mercy, erase all my sins.

—*Psalm 51:1 (ERV)*

Answer my prayers, O LORD, for your unfailing love is wonderful. Take care of me, for your mercy is so plentiful.

—*Psalm 69:16 (NLT)*

But when the kindness and love of God our Savior toward man appeared, not by works of righteousness which we have done, but according to His mercy He saved us, through the washing of regeneration and renewing of the Holy Spirit.

—*Titus 3:4–5 (NKJV)*

God's Love IS CARING

And God can give you more blessings than you need. Then you will always have plenty of everything. You will have enough to give to every good work.
—*2 Corinthians 9:8 (ERV)*

But he said to me, "My grace is sufficient for you, for my power is made perfect in weakness." Therefore I will boast all the more gladly about my weaknesses, so that Christ's power may rest on me.
—*2 Corinthians 12:9 (NIV)*

For the LORD God is our sun and our shield. He gives us grace and glory. The LORD will withhold no good thing from those who do what is right.
—*Psalm 84:11 (NLT)*

For you know the grace of our Lord Jesus Christ, that though He was rich, yet for your sakes He became poor, that you through His poverty might become rich.

—*2 Corinthians 8:9 (NKJV)*

"But I will restore you to health and heal your wounds," declares the LORD, "because you are called an outcast, Zion for whom no one cares."

—*Jeremiah 30:17 (NIV)*

But the grace (kindness) that God gives is greater. Like the Scripture says, "God is against proud people, but he gives grace (kindness) to people who are humble."

—*James 4:6 (ERV)*

But to each one of us grace was given according to the measure of Christ's gift.

—*Ephesians 4:7 (NKJV)*

For he says, "In the time of my favor I heard you, and in the day of salvation I helped you." I tell you, now is the time of God's favor, now is the day of salvation.

—*2 Corinthians 6:2 (NIV)*

Let us therefore come boldly to the throne of grace, that we may obtain mercy and find grace to help in time of need.

—*Hebrews 4:16 (NKJV)*

For he raised us from the dead along with Christ and seated us with him in the heavenly realms because we are united with Christ Jesus. So God can point to us in all future ages as examples of the incredible wealth of his grace and kindness toward us, as shown in all he has done for us who are united with Christ Jesus.

—*Ephesians 2:6–7 (NLT)*

You gave me life and were very kind to me. You cared for me and watched over my spirit.

—*Job 10:12 (ERV)*

I will look favorably upon you, making you fertile and multiplying your people. And I will fulfill my covenant with you.

—*Leviticus 26:9 (NLT)*

For You, O LORD, will bless the righteous; with favor You will surround him as with a shield.

—*Psalm 5:12 (NKJV)*

And the God of all grace, who called you to his eternal glory in Christ, after you have suffered a little while, will himself restore you and make you strong, firm and steadfast.

—*1 Peter 5:10 (NIV)*

From his abundance we have all received one gracious blessing after another.

—*John 1:16 (NLT)*

 *God's Love* NEVER FAILS

Many sorrows come to the wicked, but unfailing love surrounds those who trust the LORD.

　　　—Psalm 32:10 (NLT)

The Lord watches and cares for his followers that wait for him to show his true love.

　　　—Psalm 33:18 (ERV)

For Your mercy is great above the heavens, and Your truth reaches to the clouds.

　　　—Psalm 108:4 (NKJV)

Satisfy us each morning with your unfailing love, so we may sing for joy to the end of our lives.

　　　—Psalm 90:14 (NLT)

How priceless is your unfailing love!
Both high and low among men find
refuge in the shadow of your wings.
—Psalm 36:7 (NIV)

Praise the LORD, all you Gentiles! Laud
Him, all you peoples! For His merciful
kindness is great toward us, and the
truth of the LORD endures forever.
Praise the LORD!
—Psalm 117:1–2 (NKJV)

Your mercy, O LORD, is in the heavens;
Your faithfulness reaches to the clouds.
—Psalm 36:5 (NKJV)

I will sing forever about the Lord's love.
I will sing about his loyalty forever and
ever!
—Psalm 89:1 (ERV)

For the LORD is good; His mercy is
everlasting, and His truth endures to all
generations.
—Psalm 100:5 (NKJV)

Know therefore that the LORD your God is God; he is the faithful God, keeping his covenant of love to a thousand generations of those who love him and keep his commands.

—*Deuteronomy 7:9 (NIV)*

"For the mountains may move and the hills disappear, but even then my faithful love for you will remain. My covenant of blessing will never be broken," says the LORD, who has mercy on you.

—*Isaiah 54:10 (NLT)*

And I prayed to the LORD my God, and made confession, and said, "O Lord, great and awesome God, who keeps His covenant and mercy with those who love Him, and with those who keep His commandments."

—*Daniel 9:4 (NKJV)*

Have mercy on me, O God, according to your unfailing love; according to your great compassion blot out my transgressions.

—*Psalm 51:1 (NIV)*

But in all these things we have full victory through God who showed his love for us. Yes, I am sure that nothing can separate us from God's love—not death, not life, not angels or ruling spirits. I am sure that nothing now, nothing in the future, no powers, nothing above us or nothing below us—nothing in the whole created world—will ever be able to separate us from God's love that is in Christ Jesus our Lord.

—*Romans 8:37–39 (ERV)*

The Lord loves fairness. He will not
leave his followers without help. The
Lord will always protect his followers,
but he will destroy wicked people.
— *Psalm 37:28 (ERV)*

He calmed the storm to a whisper and
stilled the waves. What a blessing was
that stillness as he brought them safely
into harbor! Let them praise the LORD
for his great love and for the wonderful
things he has done for them.
— *Psalm 107:29–31 (NLT)*

God, in your temple we think carefully
about your loving kindness. God,
you are famous. People praise you
everywhere on earth. Everyone knows
how good you are.
— *Psalm 48:9–10 (ERV)*

Let all who fear the LORD repeat: "His
faithful love endures forever."
— *Psalm 118:4 (NLT)*

Your word, O LORD, is eternal; it stands firm in the heavens. Your faithfulness continues through all generations; you established the earth, and it endures.
—*Psalm 119:89–90 (NIV)*

Such love has no fear, because perfect love expels all fear. If we are afraid, it is for fear of punishment, and this shows that we have not fully experienced his perfect love.
—*1 John 4:18 (NLT)*

You will keep in perfect peace him whose mind is steadfast, because he trusts in you.
—*Isaiah 26:3 (NIV)*

Every good gift and every perfect gift is from above, and comes down from the Father of lights, with whom there is no variation or shadow of turning.
—*James 1:17 (NKJV)*

The Rock (the Lord)—his work is perfect! Why? Because all his ways are right! God is true and faithful. He is good and honest.

—*Deuteronomy 32:4 (ERV)*

Grace, mercy and peace from God the Father and from Jesus Christ, the Father's Son, will be with us in truth and love.

—*2 John 3 (NIV)*

LORD, don't hold back your tender mercies from me. Let your unfailing love and faithfulness always protect me.

—*Psalm 40:11 (NLT)*

Keep yourselves in the love of God, looking for the mercy of our Lord Jesus Christ unto eternal life.

—*Jude 1:21 (NKJV)*

The LORD is near to all who call on him, to all who call on him in truth.

—*Psalm 145:18 (NIV)*

Oh, thank the Lord—he is good. The Lord's love continues forever.
—*1 Chronicles 16:34 (ERV)*

Let your conduct be without covetousness; be content with such things as you have. For He Himself has said, "I will never leave you nor forsake you."
—*Hebrews 13:5 (NKJV)*

Every day the Lord shows his true love and every night, I have a song for him, a prayer for my Living God.
—*Psalm 42:8 (ERV)*

God's Love IS TRUSTWORTHY

But I pray to you, O LORD, in the time
of your favor; in your great love, O God,
answer me with your sure salvation.
>—*Psalm 69:13 (NIV)*

Trust in the LORD always, for the LORD
GOD is the eternal Rock.
>—*Isaiah 26:4 (NLT)*

He will not be afraid of evil tidings; His
heart is steadfast, trusting in the LORD.
>—*Psalm 112:7 (NKJV)*

Whenever I am afraid, I will trust in
You. In God (I will praise His word), in
God I have put my trust; I will not fear.
What can flesh do to me?
>—*Psalm 56:3–4 (NKJV)*

Praise the LORD, all you nations. Praise him, all you people of the earth. For he loves us with unfailing love; the LORD's faithfulness endures forever. Praise the LORD!

—Psalm 117:1–2 (NLT)

But the person that trusts in the Lord will be blessed. Why? Because the Lord will show him that the Lord can be trusted. That person will be strong like a tree planted near water. That tree has large roots that find the water. That tree is not afraid when the days are hot. Its leaves are always green. It does not worry in a year when no rain comes. That tree always produces fruit.

—Jeremiah 17:7–8 (ERV)

Don't let your hearts be troubled. Trust in God, and trust also in me.

—John 14:1 (NLT)

He put a new song in my mouth, a hymn of praise to our God. Many will see and fear and put their trust in the LORD.
        —*Psalm 40:3 (NIV)*

The Lord is good! His love is forever. We can trust him forever and ever!
        —*Psalm 100:5 (ERV)*

Who among you fears the LORD and obeys his servant? If you are walking in darkness, without a ray of light, trust in the LORD and rely on your God.
        —*Isaiah 50:10 (NLT)*

The law of the LORD is perfect, reviving the soul. The statutes of the LORD are trustworthy, making wise the simple.
        —*Psalm 19:7 (NIV)*

Many pains will come to bad people. But God's true love will surround the people that trust the Lord.
        —*Psalm 32:10 (ERV)*

Therefore thus says the Lord GOD:
"Behold, I lay in Zion a stone for a
foundation, a tried stone, a precious
cornerstone, a sure foundation;
whoever believes will not act hastily."
—*Isaiah 28:16 (NKJV)*

The LORD is my strength and my shield;
my heart trusts in him, and I am
helped. My heart leaps for joy and I will
give thanks to him in song.
—*Psalm 28:7 (NIV)*

Trust in the LORD, and do good;
dwell in the land, and feed on His
faithfulness. Delight yourself also in the
LORD, and He shall give you the desires
of your heart. Commit your way to the
LORD, trust also in Him, and He shall
bring it to pass.
—*Psalm 37:3–5 (NKJV)*

God's Love

HOLDS MANY PROMISES

The LORD passed in front of Moses,
calling out, "Yahweh! The LORD! The
God of compassion and mercy! I am
slow to anger and filled with unfailing
love and faithfulness. I lavish unfailing
love to a thousand generations. I forgive
iniquity, rebellion, and sin. But I do
not excuse the guilty. I lay the sins of
the parents upon their children and
grandchildren; the entire family is
affected—even children in the third and
fourth generations."
　　—Exodus 34:6–7 (NLT)

Therefore know that the LORD your
God, He is God, the faithful God
who keeps covenant and mercy for a
thousand generations with those who
love Him and keep His commandments.
　　—Deuteronomy 7:9 (NKJV)

Then I said: "O LORD, God of heaven, the great and awesome God, who keeps his covenant of love with those who love him and obey his commands."

—*Nehemiah 1:5 (NIV)*

And God raised us up with Christ and seated us with him in the heavenly realms in Christ Jesus, in order that in the coming ages he might show the incomparable riches of his grace, expressed in his kindness to us in Christ Jesus.

—*Ephesians 2:6–7 (NIV)*

We pray that the Lord Jesus Christ himself and God our Father will comfort you and strengthen you in every good thing you do and say. God loved us. Through his grace (kindness) he gave us a good hope and comfort that continues forever.

—*2 Thessalonians 2:16 (ERV)*

If you listen to these laws, and if you are careful to obey them, then the Lord your God will keep his Agreement of love with you. He promised this to your ancestors. He will love you and bless you. He will make your nation grow. He will bless your children. He will bless your fields with good crops. He will give you grain, new wine, and oil. He will bless your cows with baby calves and your sheep with lambs. You will have all these blessings in the land that he promised your ancestors to give you.

—*Deuteronomy 7:12–13 (ERV)*

But God, who is rich in mercy, because of His great love with which He loved us, even when we were dead in trespasses, made us alive together with Christ (by grace you have been saved).

—*Ephesians 2:4–5 (NKJV)*

God's Love FOR YOU

The LORD did not set his affection on you and choose you because you were more numerous than other peoples, for you were the fewest of all peoples. But it was because the LORD loved you and kept the oath he swore to your forefathers that he brought you out with a mighty hand and redeemed you from the land of slavery, from the power of Pharaoh king of Egypt. Know therefore that the LORD your God is God; he is the faithful God, keeping his covenant of love to a thousand generations of those who love him and keep his commands.

—*Deuteronomy 7:7–9 (NIV)*

Those who are led by the Spirit of God are sons of God. For you did not receive a spirit that makes you a slave again to fear, but you received the Spirit of sonship. And by him we cry, "Abba, Father." The Spirit himself testifies with our spirit that we are God's children. Now if we are children, then we are heirs—heirs of God and co-heirs with Christ, if indeed we share in his sufferings in order that we may also share in his glory.

—*Romans 8:14–17 (NIV)*

"For the mountains may move and the hills disappear, but even then my faithful love for you will remain. My covenant of blessing will never be broken," says the LORD, who has mercy on you.

—*Isaiah 54:10 (NLT)*

For I am persuaded that neither death nor life, nor angels nor principalities nor powers, nor things present nor things to come, nor height nor depth, nor any other created thing, shall be able to separate us from the love of God which is in Christ Jesus our Lord.

—*Romans 8:38–39 (NKJV)*

But you, O Lord, are a compassionate and gracious God, slow to anger, abounding in love and faithfulness.

—*Psalm 86:15 (NIV)*

For God so loved the world that He gave His only begotten Son, that whoever believes in Him should not perish but have everlasting life.

—*John 3:16 (NKJV)*

I have loved you even as the Father has loved me. Remain in my love.

—*John 15:9 (NLT)*

I pray that Christ will live in your hearts because of your faith. I pray that your life will be strong in love and be built on love. And I pray that you and all God's holy people will have the power to understand the greatness of Christ's love. I pray that you can understand how wide and how long and how high and how deep that love is. Christ's love is greater than any person can ever know. But I pray that you will be able to know that love. Then you can be filled with the fullness of God.

—*Ephesians 3:17–19 (ERV)*

Be imitators of God, therefore, as dearly loved children and live a life of love, just as Christ loved us and gave himself up for us as a fragrant offering and sacrifice to God.

—*Ephesians 5:1–2 (NIV)*

But now, O Jacob, listen to the LORD who created you. O Israel, the one who formed you says, "Do not be afraid, for I have ransomed you. I have called you by name; you are mine. When you go through deep waters, I will be with you. When you go through rivers of difficulty, you will not drown. When you walk through the fire of oppression, you will not be burned up; the flames will not consume you. For I am the LORD, your God, the Holy One of Israel, your Savior. I gave Egypt as a ransom for your freedom; I gave Ethiopia and Seba in your place. Others were given in exchange for you. I traded their lives for yours because you are precious to me. You are honored, and I love you."

—*Isaiah 43:1–4 (NLT)*

This is my commandment: Love each
other in the same way I have loved you.
There is no greater love than to lay
down one's life for one's friends.
      —*John 15:12–13 (NLT)*

The Lord said, "I love you people."
But you said, "What shows you love
us?" The Lord said, "Esau was Jacob's
brother. Right? But I chose Jacob."
      —*Malachi 1:2 (ERV)*

The LORD opens the eyes of the blind;
the LORD raises those who are bowed
down; the LORD loves the righteous.
      —*Psalm 146:8 (NKJV)*

And this hope will never disappoint
us—it will never fail. Why? Because
God has poured out his love to fill our
hearts. God gave us his love through
the Holy Spirit. That Holy Spirit was a
gift to us from God.
      —*Romans 5:5 (ERV)*

"This is the covenant I will make with the house of Israel after that time," declares the LORD. "I will put my law in their minds and write it on their hearts. I will be their God, and they will be my people. No longer will a man teach his neighbor, or a man his brother, saying, 'Know the LORD,' because they will all know me, from the least of them to the greatest," declares the LORD. "For I will forgive their wickedness and will remember their sins no more."

—*Jeremiah 31:33–34 (NIV)*

The LORD appeared to us in the past, saying: "I have loved you with an everlasting love; I have drawn you with loving-kindness."

—*Jeremiah 31:3 (NIV)*

Jesus replied, "All who love me will do what I say. My Father will love them, and we will come and make our home with each of them."
—*John 14:23 (NLT)*

This is how God showed his love to us: God sent his only Son into the world to give us life through him. True love is God's love for us, not our love for God. God sent his Son to be the way that God takes away our sins.
—*1 John 4:9–10 (ERV)*

If a person knows my commands and obeys those commands, then that person truly loves me. And my Father will love the person that loves me. And I will love that person. I will show myself to him.
—*John 14:21 (ERV)*

Yet the LORD set his affection on your forefathers and loved them, and he chose you, their descendants, above all the nations, as it is today.

—*Deuteronomy 10:15 (NIV)*

For scarcely for a righteous man will one die; yet perhaps for a good man someone would even dare to die. But God demonstrates His own love toward us, in that while we were still sinners, Christ died for us.

—*Romans 5:7–8 (NKJV)*

We know how much God loves us, and we have put our trust in his love. God is love, and all who live in love live in God, and God lives in them.

—*1 John 4:16 (NLT)*

Praise the Lord because he is good.
Sing praises to our God. It is good and
pleasant to praise him. . . . God heals
their broken hearts and bandages their
wounds. God counts the stars and
knows the name of each and every one.
Our Master is very great. He is very
powerful. There is no limit to the things
he knows. The Lord supports humble
people. But he embarrasses bad people.
. . . God fills the sky with clouds. God
makes rain for the earth. God makes
the grass grow on the mountains. God
gives food to the animals. God feeds the
young birds. War horses and powerful
soldiers don't make him happy. The
Lord is happy with people who worship
him. The Lord is pleased with people
who trust in his true love.

—*Psalm 147:1, 3–6, 8–11 (ERV)*

He chose us in Him before the foundation of the world, that we should be holy and without blame before Him in love, having predestined us to adoption as sons by Jesus Christ to Himself, according to the good pleasure of His will, to the praise of the glory of His grace, by which He made us accepted in the Beloved.

—*Ephesians 1:4–6 (NKJV)*

The Father (God) has loved us so much! This shows how much he loved us: We are called children of God. And we really are God's children. But the people in the world (people who don't believe) don't understand that we are God's children, because they have not known him (God).

—*1 John 3:1 (ERV)*

May our Lord Jesus Christ himself
and God our Father, who loved us
and by his grace gave us eternal
encouragement and good hope,
encourage your hearts and strengthen
you in every good deed and word.
    —*2 Thessalonians 2:16–17 (NIV)*

The Father Himself loves you, because
you have loved Me, and have believed
that I came forth from God.
    —*John 16:27 (NKJV)*

God's

LOVE CHANGES OUR LIVES

*Therefore, if anyone is in Christ,
he is a new creation; old things
have passed away; behold, all
things have become new.*

—2 Corinthians 5:17 (NKJV)

God's Love

Jesus told her, "I am the resurrection and the life. Anyone who believes in me will live, even after dying. Everyone who lives in me and believes in me will never ever die."

—*John 11:25–26 (NLT)*

And so we know the love that God has for us. And we trust that love. God is love. The person who lives in love lives in God. And God lives in that person. If God's love is made perfect in us, then we can be without fear on the day when God judges us. We will be without fear, because in this world we are like him (Christ or God).

—*1 John 4:16–17 (ERV)*

Then Jesus declared, "I am the bread of life. He who comes to me will never go hungry, and he who believes in me will never be thirsty."
  —*John 6:35 (NIV)*

The only temptations that you have are the same temptations that all people have. But you can trust God. He will not let you be tempted more than you can bear. But when you are tempted, God will also give you a way to escape that temptation. Then you will be able to endure it.
  —*1 Corinthians 10:13 (ERV)*

No one has ever seen God. But if we love each other, God lives in us, and his love is brought to full expression in us.
  —*1 John 4:12 (NLT)*

But whoever keeps His word, truly the love of God is perfected in him. By this we know that we are in Him.

—*1 John 2:5 (NKJV)*

Why? Because your husband is the One (God) who made you. His name is the Lord All-Powerful. He is the Protector of Israel. He is the Holy One of Israel. And he will be called the God of all the earth!

—*Isaiah 54:5 (ERV)*

Jesus answered, "Everyone who drinks this water will be thirsty again, but whoever drinks the water I give him will never thirst. Indeed, the water I give him will become in him a spring of water welling up to eternal life."

—*John 4:13–14 (NIV)*

However, as it is written: "No eye has seen, no ear has heard, no mind has conceived what God has prepared for those who love him."
—*1 Corinthians 2:9 (NIV)*

For I am persuaded that neither death nor life, nor angels nor principalities nor powers, nor things present nor things to come, nor height nor depth, nor any other created thing, shall be able to separate us from the love of God which is in Christ Jesus our Lord.
—*Romans 8:38–39 (NKJV)*

Now may our Lord Jesus Christ himself and God our Father, who loved us and by his grace gave us eternal comfort and a wonderful hope, comfort you and strengthen you in every good thing you do and say.
—*2 Thessalonians 2:16–17 (NLT)*

No, despite all these things, overwhelming victory is ours through Christ, who loved us.

—*Romans 8:37 (NLT)*

He said to me: "It is done. I am the Alpha and the Omega, the Beginning and the End. To him who is thirsty I will give to drink without cost from the spring of the water of life. He who overcomes will inherit all this, and I will be his God and he will be my son."

—*Revelation 21:6–7 (NIV)*

I said to the Lord, "Lord, you are my Master. Every good thing I have comes from you."

—*Psalm 16:2 (ERV)*

Blessed be the God and Father of our Lord Jesus Christ, who has blessed us with every spiritual blessing in the heavenly places in Christ.

—*Ephesians 1:3 (NKJV)*

For the sin of this one man, Adam, caused death to rule over many. But even greater is God's wonderful grace and his gift of righteousness, for all who receive it will live in triumph over sin and death through this one man, Jesus Christ.

—*Romans 5:17 (NLT)*

Live a life of love, just as Christ loved us and gave himself up for us as a fragrant offering and sacrifice to God.

—*Ephesians 5:2 (NIV)*

God's Love
GIVES US COMFORT

I, even I, am He who comforts you. Who
are you that you should be afraid of a
man who will die, and of the son of a
man who will be made like grass?
>—*Isaiah 51:12 (NKJV)*

Now, comfort me with your true love.
Comfort me like you promised.
>—*Psalm 119:76 (ERV)*

And God is able to make all grace
abound to you, so that in all things at
all times, having all that you need, you
will abound in every good work.
>—*2 Corinthians 9:8 (NIV)*

I will comfort you there in Jerusalem as
a mother comforts her child.
>—*Isaiah 66:13 (NLT)*

Come to me all you people that are tired and have heavy burdens. I will give you rest.
   —*Matthew 11:28 (ERV)*

Those who sow in tears shall reap in joy.
   —*Psalm 126:5 (NKJV)*

My Master, I praise you to everyone. I sing songs of praise about you to every nation. Your true love is higher than the highest clouds in the sky!
   —*Psalm 57:9–10 (ERV)*

No, I will not abandon you as orphans—I will come to you.
   —*John 14:18 (NLT)*

Cast all your anxiety on him because he cares for you.
   —*1 Peter 5:7 (NIV)*

All praise to God, the Father of our Lord Jesus Christ. God is our merciful Father and the source of all comfort. He comforts us in all our troubles so that we can comfort others. When they are troubled, we will be able to give them the same comfort God has given us. For the more we suffer for Christ, the more God will shower us with his comfort through Christ.

—*2 Corinthians 1:3–5 (NLT)*

But the Lord won't leave his people. No, the Lord was pleased to make you his own people. So, for his own good name, he won't leave you.

—*1 Samuel 12:22 (ERV)*

You will restore me to even greater honor and comfort me once again.

—*Psalm 71:21 (NLT)*

How precious are your thoughts about me, O God. They cannot be numbered! I can't even count them; they outnumber the grains of sand! And when I wake up, you are still with me!
—*Psalm 139:17–18 (NLT)*

The LORD is near to those who have a broken heart, and saves such as have a contrite spirit. Many are the afflictions of the righteous, but the LORD delivers him out of them all.
—*Psalm 34:18–19 (NKJV)*

Be strong and of good courage, do not fear nor be afraid of them; for the LORD your God, He is the One who goes with you. He will not leave you nor forsake you.
—*Deuteronomy 31:6 (NKJV)*

All he does is just and good, and all his commandments are trustworthy.
—*Psalm 111:7 (NLT)*

Even though I walk through the valley of the shadow of death, I will fear no evil, for you are with me; your rod and your staff, they comfort me.

—*Psalm 23:4 (NIV)*

"Because he loves me," says the LORD, "I will rescue him; I will protect him, for he acknowledges my name. He will call upon me, and I will answer him; I will be with him in trouble, I will deliver him and honor him."

—*Psalm 91:14–15 (NIV)*

The young women will dance for joy, and the men—old and young—will join in the celebration. I will turn their mourning into joy. I will comfort them and exchange their sorrow for rejoicing.

—*Jeremiah 31:13 (NLT)*

I was suffering, and you comforted me. Your words let me live again.

—*Psalm 119:50 (ERV)*

Those who know your name will trust in you, for you, LORD, have never forsaken those who seek you.
    —*Psalm 9:10 (NIV)*

Those who trust in the LORD are like Mount Zion, which cannot be moved, but abides forever.
    —*Psalm 125:1 (NKJV)*

The LORD is gracious and righteous; our God is full of compassion.
    —*Psalm 116:5 (NIV)*

Everything the Lord does is good. Everything he does shows how good he is.
    —*Psalm 145:17 (ERV)*

I, the LORD, have called You in righteousness, and will hold Your hand; I will keep You and give You as a covenant to the people, as a light to the Gentiles.
    —*Isaiah 42:6 (NKJV)*

The salvation of the righteous comes from the LORD; he is their stronghold in time of trouble.
—*Psalm 37:39 (NIV)*

Don't be afraid, for I am with you. Don't be discouraged, for I am your God. I will strengthen you and help you. I will hold you up with my victorious right hand.
—*Isaiah 41:10 (NLT)*

The LORD executes righteousness and justice for all who are oppressed.
—*Psalm 103:6 (NKJV)*

God makes people right through their faith in Jesus Christ. God does this for all people that believe in Christ. All people are the same.
—*Romans 3:22 (ERV)*

The thief's purpose is to steal and kill and destroy. My purpose is to give them a rich and satisfying life.
—*John 10:10 (NLT)*

My dear children, I write this to you so that you will not sin. But if anybody does sin, we have one who speaks to the Father in our defense—Jesus Christ, the Righteous One.

—*1 John 2:1 (NIV)*

And if I go and prepare a place for you, I will come again and receive you to Myself; that where I am, there you may be also.

—*John 14:3 (NKJV)*

When you go through deep waters, I will be with you. When you go through rivers of difficulty, you will not drown. When you walk through the fire of oppression, you will not be burned up; the flames will not consume you.

—*Isaiah 43:2 (NLT)*

So all of you should live together in peace. Try to understand each other. Love each other like brothers. Be kind and humble.

—*1 Peter 3:8 (ERV)*

And Jesus said to them, "I am the bread of life. He who comes to Me shall never hunger, and he who believes in Me shall never thirst."

—*John 6:35 (NKJV)*

When Jesus spoke again to the people, he said, "I am the light of the world. Whoever follows me will never walk in darkness, but will have the light of life."

—*John 8:12 (NIV)*

For the word of the LORD is right, and all His work is done in truth.

—*Psalm 33:4 (NKJV)*

God's Love
RELIEVES OUR FEARS

Where God's love is, there is no fear. Why? Because God's perfect love takes away fear. It is God's punishment that makes a person fear. So God's love is not made perfect in the person who has fear.

> —*1 John 4:18 (ERV)*

Don't be afraid, for I am with you. Don't be discouraged, for I am your God. I will strengthen you and help you. I will hold you up with my victorious right hand.

> —*Isaiah 41:10 (NLT)*

For you did not receive a spirit that makes you a slave again to fear, but you received the Spirit of sonship. And by him we cry, "Abba, Father."

> —*Romans 8:15 (NIV)*

I went to God for help. And he listened.
He saved me from all the things I fear.
—*Psalm 34:4 (ERV)*

Yea, though I walk through the valley of
the shadow of death, I will fear no evil;
for You are with me; Your rod and Your
staff, they comfort me.
—*Psalm 23:4 (NKJV)*

Why? Because you trust the Lord. You
made God Most-High your place of
safety. Nothing bad will happen to you.
There will be no diseases in your home.
God will command his angels for you,
and they will protect you wherever you go.
—*Psalm 91:9–11 (ERV)*

Cast your cares on the LORD and he
will sustain you; he will never let the
righteous fall.
—*Psalm 55:22 (NIV)*

But I will call on God, and the LORD will rescue me. Morning, noon, and night I cry out in my distress, and the LORD hears my voice.

—*Psalm 55:16–17 (NLT)*

And we know that in all things God works for the good of those who love him, who have been called according to his purpose. . . . What, then, shall we say in response to this? If God is for us, who can be against us? He who did not spare his own Son, but gave him up for us all—how will he not also, along with him, graciously give us all things?

—*Romans 8:28, 31–32 (NIV)*

So be strong and courageous! Do not be afraid and do not panic before them. For the LORD your God will personally go ahead of you. He will neither fail you nor abandon you.

—*Deuteronomy 31:6 (NLT)*

Jacob, the Lord made you! Israel, the Lord made you! And now the Lord says, "Don't be afraid! I saved you. I named you. You are mine. When you have troubles, I am with you. When you cross rivers, you will not be hurt. When you walk through fire, you will not be burned; the flames will not hurt you."
—*Isaiah 43:1–2 (ERV)*

Fear is like a trap. But if you trust in the Lord, you will be safe.
—*Proverbs 29:25 (ERV)*

And he said, "Listen, all you of Judah and you inhabitants of Jerusalem, and you, King Jehoshaphat! Thus says the LORD to you: 'Do not be afraid nor dismayed because of this great multitude, for the battle is not yours, but God's.'"
—*2 Chronicles 20:15 (NKJV)*

It is good for a person to be kind and generous. It is good for a person to be fair in his business. That person will never fall. A good person will be remembered forever. He will not be afraid of bad news. That person is confident because he trusts the Lord. That person is confident. He will not be afraid. He will defeat his enemies.

—*Psalm 112:5–8 (ERV)*

The LORD himself goes before you and will be with you; he will never leave you nor forsake you. Do not be afraid; do not be discouraged.

—*Deuteronomy 31:8 (NIV)*

Peace I leave with you; my peace I give you. I do not give to you as the world gives. Do not let your hearts be troubled and do not be afraid.

—*John 14:27 (NIV)*

For I know the thoughts that I think toward you, says the LORD, thoughts of peace and not of evil, to give you a future and a hope. Then you will call upon Me and go and pray to Me, and I will listen to you. And you will seek Me and find Me, when you search for Me with all your heart.

—*Jeremiah 29:11–13 (NKJV)*

Give all your worries and cares to God, for he cares about you.

—*1 Peter 5:7 (NLT)*

God's Love
OFFERS US SECURITY

You can go to God Most-High to hide.
You can go to the God All-Powerful for
protection.
  —Psalm 91:1 (ERV)

You are my hiding place; You shall
preserve me from trouble; You shall
surround me with songs of deliverance.
  —Psalm 32:7 (NKJV)

The LORD is my rock and my fortress
and my deliverer; my God, my strength,
in whom I will trust; my shield and the
horn of my salvation, my stronghold. I
will call upon the LORD, who is worthy
to be praised; so shall I be saved from
my enemies.
  —Psalm 18:2–3 (NKJV)

The LORD is a refuge for the oppressed,
a stronghold in times of trouble.
    —*Psalm 9:9 (NIV)*

But let all who take refuge in you
rejoice; let them sing joyful praises
forever. Spread your protection over
them, that all who love your name may
be filled with joy.
    —*Psalm 5:11 (NLT)*

The LORD is good, a stronghold in the
day of trouble; and He knows those who
trust in Him.
    —*Nahum 1:7 (NKJV)*

The Lord will protect that person and
save his life. That person will be blessed
on earth. God will not let that person's
enemies destroy him.
    —*Psalm 41:2 (ERV)*

May the LORD answer you when you
are in distress; may the name of the
God of Jacob protect you.
        —*Psalm 20:1 (NIV)*

I know the LORD is always with me. I
will not be shaken, for he is right beside
me. No wonder my heart is glad, and I
rejoice. My body rests in safety.
        —*Psalm 16:8–9 (NLT)*

God is our refuge and strength, a very
present help in trouble.
        —*Psalm 46:1 (NKJV)*

May integrity and honesty protect me,
for I put my hope in you.
        —*Psalm 25:21 (NLT)*

The eternal God is your refuge, and
underneath are the everlasting arms.
He will drive out your enemy before
you, saying, "Destroy him!"
        —*Deuteronomy 33:27 (NIV)*

No, my share and my cup come only from the Lord. Lord, you support me. You give me my share.
        —*Psalm 16:5 (ERV)*

For in the time of trouble He shall hide me in His pavilion; in the secret place of His tabernacle He shall hide me; He shall set me high upon a rock.
        —*Psalm 27:5 (NKJV)*

I give them eternal life, and they shall never perish; no one can snatch them out of my hand.
        —*John 10:28 (NIV)*

God's Love

BRINGS US CONTENTMENT

Earth, sing to the Lord! Be happy as you serve the Lord! Come before the Lord with happy songs! Know that the Lord is God. He made us. We are his people, we are his sheep.

—Psalm 100:1–3 (ERV)

Though the fig tree may not blossom, nor fruit be on the vines; though the labor of the olive may fail, and the fields yield no food; though the flock may be cut off from the fold, and there be no herd in the stalls—yet I will rejoice in the LORD, I will joy in the God of my salvation.

—Habakkuk 3:17–18 (NKJV)

Take delight in the LORD, and he will give you your heart's desires.

—Psalm 37:4 (NLT)

You will show me the path of life; in Your presence is fullness of joy; at Your right hand are pleasures forevermore.

—*Psalm 16:11 (NKJV)*

The Lord is my strength. He is my shield. I trusted him. And he helped me. I am very happy! And I sing songs of praise to him.

—*Psalm 28:7 (ERV)*

Clap your hands, all you nations; shout to God with cries of joy. How awesome is the LORD Most High, the great King over all the earth!

—*Psalm 47:1–2 (NIV)*

For the LORD your God is living among you. He is a mighty savior. He will take delight in you with gladness. With his love, he will calm all your fears. He will rejoice over you with joyful songs.

—*Zephaniah 3:17 (NLT)*

Honor and majesty surround him;
strength and joy fill his dwelling. O
nations of the world, recognize the
LORD, recognize that the LORD is
glorious and strong.
—*1 Chronicles 16:27–28 (NLT)*

The Lord makes me very, very happy.
My whole self is happy in my God. The
Lord put the clothes of salvation on me.
These clothes are like the nice clothes
a man wears at his wedding. The Lord
put the coat of goodness on me. This
coat is like the beautiful clothes a
woman wears at her wedding. The earth
causes plants to grow. People plant
seeds in the garden, and the garden
makes them grow. In the same way, the
Lord will make goodness grow. The Lord
will make praise grow in all the nations.
—*Isaiah 61:10–11 (ERV)*

God's Love

OFFERS US FORGIVENESS

They refused to listen and failed to remember the miracles you performed among them. They became stiff-necked and in their rebellion appointed a leader in order to return to their slavery. But you are a forgiving God, gracious and compassionate, slow to anger and abounding in love. Therefore you did not desert them.

—*Nehemiah 9:17 (NIV)*

This wine is my blood. My blood (death) begins the new agreement from God to his people. This blood is given for many people to forgive their sins.

—*Matthew 26:28 (ERV)*

But if we confess our sins to him, he is faithful and just to forgive us our sins and to cleanse us from all wickedness.

—*1 John 1:9 (NLT)*

Purge me with hyssop, and I shall be clean; wash me, and I shall be whiter than snow. Make me hear joy and gladness, that the bones You have broken may rejoice. Hide Your face from my sins, and blot out all my iniquities. Create in me a clean heart, O God, and renew a steadfast spirit within me.
—*Psalm 51:7–10 (NKJV)*

So now people that are in Christ Jesus are not judged guilty. Why? Because in Christ Jesus the law of the Spirit that brings life made you free. It made you free from the law that brings sin and death.
—*Romans 8:1–2 (ERV)*

In Him we have redemption through His blood, the forgiveness of sins, according to the riches of His grace.
—*Ephesians 1:7 (NKJV)*

Forget the former things; do not dwell
on the past. See, I am doing a new
thing! Now it springs up; do you not
perceive it? I am making a way in the
desert and streams in the wasteland.

—*Isaiah 43:18–19 (NIV)*

Most of those who came from Ephraim,
Manasseh, Issachar, and Zebulun
had not purified themselves. But King
Hezekiah prayed for them, and they
were allowed to eat the Passover meal
anyway, even though this was contrary
to the requirements of the Law. For
Hezekiah said, "May the LORD, who is
good, pardon those who decide to follow
the LORD, the God of their ancestors,
even though they are not properly
cleansed for the ceremony."

—*2 Chronicles 30:18–19 (NLT)*

People who conceal their sins will not prosper, but if they confess and turn from them, they will receive mercy.
—*Proverbs 28:13 (NLT)*

My soul, praise the Lord! And don't forget that he is truly kind. God forgives us for all the sins we do. He heals all our sicknesses.
—*Psalm 103:2–3 (ERV)*

Our God and Savior, help us! Help us! Save us! That will bring glory to your name. Erase our sins for the good of your name.
—*Psalm 79:9 (ERV)*

He has delivered us from the power of darkness and conveyed us into the kingdom of the Son of His love, in whom we have redemption through His blood, the forgiveness of sins.
—*Colossians 1:13–14 (NKJV)*

Let the wicked forsake his way and the evil man his thoughts. Let him turn to the LORD, and he will have mercy on him, and to our God, for he will freely pardon.

—*Isaiah 55:7 (NIV)*

No more shall every man teach his neighbor, and every man his brother, saying, "Know the LORD," for they all shall know Me, from the least of them to the greatest of them, says the LORD. For I will forgive their iniquity, and their sin I will remember no more.

—*Jeremiah 31:34 (NKJV)*

So you must change your hearts and lives! Come back to God and he will forgive your sins.

—*Acts 3:19 (ERV)*

For his unfailing love toward those who fear him is as great as the height of the heavens above the earth. He has removed our sins as far from us as the east is from the west.

—*Psalm 103:11–12 (NLT)*

For God so loved the world that he gave his one and only Son, that whoever believes in him shall not perish but have eternal life. For God did not send his Son into the world to condemn the world, but to save the world through him.

—*John 3:16–17 (NIV)*

LORD, if you kept a record of our sins, who, O Lord, could ever survive? But you offer forgiveness, that we might learn to fear you. I am counting on the LORD; yes, I am counting on him. I have put my hope in his word.

—*Psalm 130:3–5 (NLT)*

To You, O my Strength, I will sing praises; for God is my defense, my God of mercy.

> —*Psalm 59:17 (NKJV)*

The LORD is my strength and my shield; my heart trusts in him, and I am helped. My heart leaps for joy and I will give thanks to him in song.

> —*Psalm 28:7 (NIV)*

The name of the LORD is a strong fortress; the godly run to him and are safe.

> —*Proverbs 18:10 (NLT)*

The LORD is my strength and my song; he has become my salvation. He is my God, and I will praise him, my father's God, and I will exalt him.

> —*Exodus 15:2 (NIV)*

Nehemiah said, "Go and enjoy the good food and sweet drinks. And give some food and drinks to those people that didn't prepare any food. Today is a special day to the Lord. Don't be sad! Why? Because the joy of the Lord will make you strong."

—*Nehemiah 8:10 (ERV)*

My shield is God Most High, who saves the upright in heart.

—*Psalm 7:10 (NIV)*

What then shall we say to these things? If God is for us, who can be against us?

—*Romans 8:31 (NKJV)*

Wealth and honor come from you alone, for you rule over everything. Power and might are in your hand, and at your discretion people are made great and given strength.

—*1 Chronicles 29:12 (NLT)*

My flesh and my heart may fail, but God is the strength of my heart and my portion forever.

—*Psalm 73:26 (NIV)*

He said, "Lord my strength, I love you!"

—*Psalm 18:1 (ERV)*

The LORD will give strength to His people; the LORD will bless His people with peace.

—*Psalm 29:11 (NKJV)*

In his kindness God called you to share in his eternal glory by means of Christ Jesus. So after you have suffered a little while, he will restore, support, and strengthen you, and he will place you on a firm foundation.

—*1 Peter 5:10 (NLT)*

I can do all things through Christ, because he gives me strength.

—*Philippians 4:13 (ERV)*

Do you not know? Have you not heard? The LORD is the everlasting God, the Creator of the ends of the earth. He will not grow tired or weary, and his understanding no one can fathom. He gives strength to the weary and increases the power of the weak. Even youths grow tired and weary, and young men stumble and fall; but those who hope in the LORD will renew their strength. They will soar on wings like eagles; they will run and not grow weary, they will walk and not be faint.
—*Isaiah 40:28–31 (NIV)*

Praise be to the Lord, to God our Savior, who daily bears our burdens.
—*Psalm 68:19 (NIV)*

God's Love

Jeremiah, I am the Lord. I am the God of every person on the earth. Jeremiah, you know that nothing is impossible for me.

—Jeremiah 32:27 (ERV)

And this same God who takes care of me will supply all your needs from his glorious riches, which have been given to us in Christ Jesus.

—Philippians 4:19 (NLT)

For the LORD God is a sun and shield; the LORD bestows favor and honor; no good thing does he withhold from those whose walk is blameless.

—Psalm 84:11 (NIV)

Bless the LORD, O my soul, and forget
not all His benefits: . . . Who redeems
your life from destruction, Who crowns
you with lovingkindness and tender
mercies, Who satisfies your mouth
with good things, so that your youth is
renewed like the eagle's.
    —*Psalm 103:2, 4–5 (NKJV)*

God gives food to his followers. God
remembers his Agreement forever.
    —*Psalm 111:5 (ERV)*

Continue to ask, and God will give
to you. Continue to search, and you
will find. Continue to knock, and the
door will open for you. Yes, if a person
continues asking, that person will
receive. If a person continues looking,
that person will find. And if a person
continues knocking, the door will open
for that person.
    —*Matthew 7:7–8 (ERV)*

I will bless my people and their homes around my holy hill. And in the proper season I will send the showers they need. There will be showers of blessing. The orchards and fields of my people will yield bumper crops, and everyone will live in safety. When I have broken their chains of slavery and rescued them from those who enslaved them, then they will know that I am the LORD.

—*Ezekiel 34:26–27 (NLT)*

"Bring all the tithes into the storehouse, that there may be food in My house, and try Me now in this," says the LORD of hosts, "If I will not open for you the windows of heaven and pour out for you such blessing that there will not be room enough to receive it."

—*Malachi 3:10 (NKJV)*

Then I said, "LORD, you know what's happening to me. Please step in and help me. Punish my persecutors! Please give me time; don't let me die young. It's for your sake that I am suffering."
—*Jeremiah 15:15 (NLT)*

But God was always there doing things that prove he is real. He gives you rain from the sky. He gives you good harvests at the right times. He gives you plenty of food, and he fills your hearts with joy.
—*Acts 14:17 (ERV)*

Command those who are rich in this present world not to be arrogant nor to put their hope in wealth, which is so uncertain, but to put their hope in God, who richly provides us with everything for our enjoyment.
—*1 Timothy 6:17 (NIV)*

You open Your hand and satisfy the desire of every living thing.
>   —*Psalm 145:16 (NKJV)*

Enjoy serving the Lord, and he will give you what you want.
>   —*Psalm 37:4 (ERV)*

Whom have I in heaven but You? And there is none upon earth that I desire besides You. My flesh and my heart fail; but God is the strength of my heart and my portion forever.
>   —*Psalm 73:25–26 (NKJV)*

For none of us lives to himself alone and none of us dies to himself alone. If we live, we live to the Lord; and if we die, we die to the Lord. So, whether we live or die, we belong to the Lord.
>   —*Romans 14:7–8 (NIV)*

O LORD, you have searched me and you know me. You know when I sit and when I rise; you perceive my thoughts from afar. You discern my going out and my lying down; you are familiar with all my ways. Before a word is on my tongue you know it completely, O LORD.

You hem me in—behind and before; you have laid your hand upon me. Such knowledge is too wonderful for me, too lofty for me to attain.

Where can I go from your Spirit? Where can I flee from your presence? If I go up to the heavens, you are there; if I make my bed in the depths, you are there. If I rise on the wings of the dawn, if I settle on the far side of the sea, even there your hand will guide me, your right hand will hold me fast.

—*Psalm 139:1–10 (NIV)*

But if you remain in me and my words remain in you, you may ask for anything you want, and it will be granted!

—*John 15:7 (NLT)*

The LORD is my shepherd; I shall not want.

—*Psalm 23:1 (NKJV)*

God's Love GIVES REST

I will lie down and sleep in peace, for you alone, O LORD, make me dwell in safety.

> —*Psalm 4:8 (NIV)*

I wait quietly before God, for my victory comes from him. He alone is my rock and my salvation, my fortress where I will never be shaken.

> —*Psalm 62:1–2 (NLT)*

Young men become tired and need to rest. Even young boys stumble and fall. But people that trust the Lord become strong again like eagles that grow new feathers. These people run without becoming weak. These people walk without becoming tired.

> —*Isaiah 40:30–31 (ERV)*

Don't worry, I am with you. Don't be afraid, I am your God. I will make you strong. I will help you. I will support you with my good right hand.

—Isaiah 41:10 (ERV)

[Cast] all your care upon Him, for He cares for you.

—1 Peter 5:7 (NKJV)

The LORD gives his people strength. The LORD blesses them with peace.

—Psalm 29:11 (NLT)

God lives forever. He is your place of safety. God's power continues forever! He is protecting you. God will force your enemies to leave your land. He will say, "Destroy the enemy!"

—Deuteronomy 33:27 (ERV)

Cast your cares on the LORD and he will sustain you; he will never let the righteous fall.

—Psalm 55:22 (NIV)

They were in trouble, so they called to the Lord for help. And he saved them from their troubles. God stopped the storm. He calmed the waves. The sailors were happy that the sea was calm. And God led them safely to the place they wanted to go. Thank the Lord for his love, and for the amazing things he does for people.

—Psalm 107:28–31 (ERV)

Moses said this about the tribe of Benjamin: "The people of Benjamin are loved by the LORD and live in safety beside him. He surrounds them continuously and preserves them from every harm."

—Deuteronomy 33:12 (NLT)

Praise be to the Lord, to God our Savior, who daily bears our burdens.

—Psalm 68:19 (NIV)

The LORD is my shepherd, I shall not be in want. He makes me lie down in green pastures, he leads me beside quiet waters, he restores my soul. He guides me in paths of righteousness for his name's sake.

—*Psalm 23:1–3 (NIV)*

I waited patiently for the LORD to help me, and he turned to me and heard my cry. He lifted me out of the pit of despair, out of the mud and the mire. He set my feet on solid ground and steadied me as I walked along. He has given me a new song to sing, a hymn of praise to our God. Many will see what he has done and be amazed. They will put their trust in the LORD.

—*Psalm 40:1–3 (NLT)*

My soul follows close behind You; Your right hand upholds me.

—*Psalm 63:8 (NKJV)*

I was very worried and upset. But Lord, you comforted me and made me happy!
—*Psalm 94:19 (ERV)*

The name of the LORD is a strong fortress; the godly run to him and are safe.
—*Proverbs 18:10 (NLT)*

When you pass through the waters, I will be with you; and when you pass through the rivers, they will not sweep over you. When you walk through the fire, you will not be burned; the flames will not set you ablaze.
—*Isaiah 43:2 (NIV)*

Thus says the LORD: "Stand in the ways and see, and ask for the old paths, where the good way is, and walk in it; then you will find rest for your souls. But they said, 'We will not walk in it.'"
—*Jeremiah 6:16 (NKJV)*

The Lord says, "The mountains may disappear, and the hills may become dust. But my kindness will never leave you. I will make peace with you, and it will never end." The Lord shows mercy to you. And he is the One that said these things.

—*Isaiah 54:10 (ERV)*

Come, let us bow down in worship, let us kneel before the LORD our Maker; for he is our God and we are the people of his pasture, the flock under his care.

—*Psalm 95:6–7 (NIV)*

I will refresh the weary and satisfy the faint.

—*Jeremiah 31:25 (NIV)*

Peace I leave with you, My peace I give to you; not as the world gives do I give to you. Let not your heart be troubled, neither let it be afraid.

—*John 14:27 (NKJV)*

Find rest, O my soul, in God alone; my hope comes from him.

  —Psalm 62:5 (NIV)

Come to me all you people that are tired and have heavy burdens. I will give you rest. Accept my work and learn from me. I am gentle and humble in spirit. And you will find rest for your souls. Yes, the work that I ask you to accept is easy. The burden I give you to carry is not heavy.

  —Matthew 11:28–30 (ERV)

Don't let your hearts be troubled. Trust in God, and trust also in me.

  —John 14:1 (NLT)

I will not leave you all alone like children without parents. I will come back to you.

  —John 14:18 (ERV)

Be anxious for nothing, but in everything by prayer and supplication, with thanksgiving, let your requests be made known to God; and the peace of God, which surpasses all understanding, will guard your hearts and minds through Christ Jesus.

—Philippians 4:6–7 (NKJV)

I told you these things so that you can have peace in me. In this world you will have trouble. But be brave! I have defeated the world!

—John 16:33 (ERV)

D'S PROMIS PROM

CALLS US TO LOVE

We should love one another.

—1 John 3:11 (NLT)

Jesus replied: "Love the Lord your God with all your heart and with all your soul and with all your mind."

—*Matthew 22:37 (NIV)*

Therefore take careful heed to yourselves, that you love the LORD your God.

—*Joshua 23:11 (NKJV)*

I love the LORD because he hears my voice and my prayer for mercy.

—*Psalm 116:1 (NLT)*

As the deer pants for the water brooks, so pants my soul for You, O God.

—*Psalm 42:1 (NKJV)*

Loving GOD

Oh, love the LORD, all you His saints! For the LORD preserves the faithful, and fully repays the proud person.

—*Psalm 31:23 (NKJV)*

If you love me, then you will do the things I command. . . . If a person knows my commands and obeys those commands, then that person truly loves me. And my Father will love the person that loves me. And I will love that person. I will show myself to him.

—*John 14:15, 21 (ERV)*

The Lord protects every person who loves him. But the Lord destroys bad people.

—*Psalm 145:20 (ERV)*

Great peace have they who love your law, and nothing can make them stumble.
—*Psalm 119:165 (NIV)*

Come, let us worship and bow down. Let us kneel before the LORD our maker, for he is our God. We are the people he watches over, the flock under his care. If only you would listen to his voice today!
—*Psalm 95:6–7 (NLT)*

Because he has set his love upon Me, therefore I will deliver him; I will set him on high, because he has known My name. He shall call upon Me, and I will answer him; I will be with him in trouble; I will deliver him and honor him. With long life I will satisfy him, and show him My salvation.
—*Psalm 91:14–16 (NKJV)*

And we know that God causes everything to work together for the good of those who love God and are called according to his purpose for them.
—*Romans 8:28 (NLT)*

However, as it is written: "No eye has seen, no ear has heard, no mind has conceived what God has prepared for those who love him."
—*1 Corinthians 2:9 (NIV)*

What great blessings there are for the person who is tempted and still continues strong. Why? Because after he has proved his faith, God will give him the reward of life forever. God promised this to all people who love him.
—*James 1:12 (ERV)*

We love Him because He first loved us.
—*1 John 4:19 (NKJV)*

Loving ONE ANOTHER

Beloved, if God so loved us, we also ought to love one another. No one has seen God at any time. If we love one another, God abides in us, and His love has been perfected in us.

—*1 John 4:11–12 (NKJV)*

And he (God) gave us this command: The person who loves God must also love his brothers and sisters in Christ.

—*1 John 4:21 (ERV)*

Every time I think of you, I give thanks to my God. Whenever I pray, I make my requests for all of you with joy, for you have been my partners in spreading the Good News about Christ from the time you first heard it until now.

—*Philippians 1:3–5 (NLT)*

Greater love has no one than this, that he lay down his life for his friends.
    —*John 15:13 (NIV)*

Finally, all of you be of one mind, having compassion for one another; love as brothers, be tenderhearted, be courteous.
    —*1 Peter 3:8 (NKJV)*

For the whole law can be summed up in this one command: "Love your neighbor as yourself."
    —*Galatians 5:14 (NLT)*

Now that you have purified yourselves by obeying the truth so that you have sincere love for your brothers, love one another deeply, from the heart.
    —*1 Peter 1:22 (NIV)*

And let us consider how we may spur one another on toward love and good deeds.
    —*Hebrews 10:24 (NIV)*

Let no debt remain outstanding, except the continuing debt to love one another, for he who loves his fellowman has fulfilled the law. The commandments, "Do not commit adultery," "Do not murder," "Do not steal," "Do not covet," and whatever other commandment there may be, are summed up in this one rule: "Love your neighbor as yourself." Love does no harm to its neighbor. Therefore love is the fulfillment of the law.

—*Romans 13:8–10 (NIV)*

Dear friends, we should love each other, because love comes from God. The person who loves has become God's child. And so the person who loves knows God.

—*1 John 4:7 (ERV)*

Let brotherly love continue.

—*Hebrews 13:1 (NKJV)*

This is how we know that we love the children of God: by loving God and carrying out his commands. This is love for God: to obey his commands. And his commands are not burdensome.

—*1 John 5:2–3 (NIV)*

But we don't need to write to you about the importance of loving each other, for God himself has taught you to love one another.

—*1 Thessalonians 4:9 (NLT)*

Honor all people. Love the brotherhood. Fear God. Honor the king.

—*1 Peter 2:17 (NKJV)*

The man answered, "'You must love the Lord your God. You must love him with all your heart, all your soul, all your strength, and all your mind.' Also, 'You must love other people the same as you love yourself.'"

—*Luke 10:27 (ERV)*

Loving GOD

Oh, love the LORD, all you His saints!
For the LORD preserves the faithful, and
fully repays the proud person.
—*Psalm 31:23 (NKJV)*

If you love me, then you will do the
things I command. . . . If a person
knows my commands and obeys those
commands, then that person truly loves
me. And my Father will love the person
that loves me. And I will love that
person. I will show myself to him.
—*John 14:15, 21 (ERV)*

The Lord protects every person who
loves him. But the Lord destroys bad
people.
—*Psalm 145:20 (ERV)*

Great peace have they who love your law, and nothing can make them stumble.
—*Psalm 119:165 (NIV)*

Come, let us worship and bow down. Let us kneel before the LORD our maker, for he is our God. We are the people he watches over, the flock under his care. If only you would listen to his voice today!
—*Psalm 95:6–7 (NLT)*

Because he has set his love upon Me, therefore I will deliver him; I will set him on high, because he has known My name. He shall call upon Me, and I will answer him; I will be with him in trouble; I will deliver him and honor him. With long life I will satisfy him, and show him My salvation.
—*Psalm 91:14–16 (NKJV)*

And we know that God causes everything to work together for the good of those who love God and are called according to his purpose for them.

—*Romans 8:28 (NLT)*

However, as it is written: "No eye has seen, no ear has heard, no mind has conceived what God has prepared for those who love him."

—*1 Corinthians 2:9 (NIV)*

What great blessings there are for the person who is tempted and still continues strong. Why? Because after he has proved his faith, God will give him the reward of life forever. God promised this to all people who love him.

—*James 1:12 (ERV)*

We love Him because He first loved us.

—*1 John 4:19 (NKJV)*

Jesus replied: "Love the Lord your God with all your heart and with all your soul and with all your mind."

  —Matthew 22:37 (NIV)

Therefore take careful heed to yourselves, that you love the LORD your God.

  —Joshua 23:11 (NKJV)

I love the LORD because he hears my voice and my prayer for mercy.

  —Psalm 116:1 (NLT)

As the deer pants for the water brooks, so pants my soul for You, O God.

  —Psalm 42:1 (NKJV)

Is there any encouragement from belonging to Christ? Any comfort from his love? Any fellowship together in the Spirit? Are your hearts tender and compassionate? Then make me truly happy by agreeing wholeheartedly with each other, loving one another, and working together with one mind and purpose.

—Philippians 2:1–2 (NLT)

Do not seek revenge or bear a grudge against a fellow Israelite, but love your neighbor as yourself. I am the LORD.

—Leviticus 19:18 (NLT)

We pray that the Lord will make your love grow. We pray that he will give you more and more love for each other and for all people. We pray that you will love all people like we love you.

—1 Thessalonians 3:12 (ERV)

Now brothers and sisters, we ask you to respect those people who work hard with you—those who lead you in the Lord and teach you. Respect those people with a very special love because of the work they do with you. Live in peace with each other.

—*1 Thessalonians 5:12–13 (ERV)*

Most important of all, continue to show deep love for each other, for love covers a multitude of sins.

—*1 Peter 4:8 (NLT)*

We ought always to thank God for you, brothers, and rightly so, because your faith is growing more and more, and the love every one of you has for each other is increasing.

—*2 Thessalonians 1:3 (NIV)*

I, therefore, the prisoner of the Lord, beseech you to walk worthy of the calling with which you were called, with all lowliness and gentleness, with longsuffering, bearing with one another in love, endeavoring to keep the unity of the Spirit in the bond of peace.

—*Ephesians 4:1–3 (NKJV)*

Love is patient, love is kind. It does not envy, it does not boast, it is not proud. It is not rude, it is not self-seeking, it is not easily angered, it keeps no record of wrongs. Love does not delight in evil but rejoices with the truth. It always protects, always trusts, always hopes, always perseveres. Love never fails. But where there are prophecies, they will cease; where there are tongues, they will be stilled; where there is knowledge, it will pass away.

—*1 Corinthians 13:4–8 (NIV)*

If you really fulfill the royal law according to the Scripture, "You shall love your neighbor as yourself," you do well.

—*James 2:8 (NKJV)*

Hate causes arguments. But love forgives every wrong thing people do.
  —*Proverbs 10:12 (ERV)*

God has chosen you and made you his holy people. He loves you. So always do these things: Show mercy to people; be kind, humble, gentle, and patient. Don't be angry with each other, but forgive each other. If another person does something wrong against you, then forgive that person. Forgive other people because the Lord forgave you. Do all these things; but most important, love each other. Love is the thing that holds you all together in perfect unity.
  —*Colossians 3:12–14 (ERV)*

May the Lord make your love increase
and overflow for each other and for
everyone else, just as ours does for you.
—*1 Thessalonians 3:12 (NIV)*

See that no one pays back evil for evil,
but always try to do good to each other
and to all people.
—*1 Thessalonians 5:15 (NLT)*

But Ruth replied, "Don't urge me to
leave you or to turn back from you.
Where you go I will go, and where you
stay I will stay. Your people will be my
people and your God my God. Where
you die I will die, and there I will be
buried. May the LORD deal with me, be
it ever so severely, if anything but death
separates you and me."
—*Ruth 1:16–17 (NIV)*

And let us consider one another in
order to stir up love and good works.
—*Hebrews 10:24 (NKJV)*

[Speak to] the older women likewise, that they be reverent in behavior, not slanderers, not given to much wine, teachers of good things—that they admonish the young women to love their husbands, to love their children.
—*Titus 2:3–4 (NKJV)*

And let us consider one another in order to stir up love and good works.
—*Hebrews 10:24 (NKJV)*

Love the LORD your God with all your heart and with all your soul and with all your strength. These commandments that I give you today are to be upon your hearts. Impress them on your children. Talk about them when you sit at home and when you walk along the road, when you lie down and when you get up.
—*Deuteronomy 6:5–7 (NIV)*

As a father has compassion on his children, so the LORD has compassion on those who fear him.

—*Psalm 103:13 (NIV)*

Teach a child the right way to live while he is young. Then when he grows older, he will continue living that way.

—*Proverbs 22:6 (ERV)*

So let's stop condemning each other. Decide instead to live in such a way that you will not cause another believer to stumble and fall.

—*Romans 14:13 (NLT)*

However, each one of you also must love his wife as he loves himself, and the wife must respect her husband.

—*Ephesians 5:33 (NIV)*

Two people are better off than one, for they can help each other succeed. If one person falls, the other can reach out and help. But someone who falls alone is in real trouble.

—*Ecclesiastes 4:9–10 (NLT)*

Loving YOUR FRIENDS

Love suffers long and is kind; love does not envy; love does not parade itself, is not puffed up; does not behave rudely, does not seek its own, is not provoked, thinks no evil; does not rejoice in iniquity, but rejoices in the truth; bears all things, believes all things, hopes all things, endures all things. Love never fails. But whether there are prophecies, they will fail; whether there are tongues, they will cease; whether there is knowledge, it will vanish away.

—*1 Corinthians 13:4–8 (NKJV)*

Greater love has no one than this, that he lay down his life for his friends. You are my friends if you do what I command.

—*John 15:13–14 (NIV)*

Wounds from a sincere friend are better than many kisses from an enemy.
>—*Proverbs 27:6 (NLT)*

My friends scorn me, but I pour out my tears to God. I need someone to mediate between God and me, as a person mediates between friends.
>—*Job 16:20–21 (NLT)*

For you have been called to live in freedom, my brothers and sisters. But don't use your freedom to satisfy your sinful nature. Instead, use your freedom to serve one another in love.
>—*Galatians 5:13 (NLT)*

We pray that the Lord will make your love grow. We pray that he will give you more and more love for each other and for all people. We pray that you will love all people like we love you.
>—*1 Thessalonians 3:12 (ERV)*

Do not forsake your own friend or your father's friend, nor go to your brother's house in the day of your calamity; better is a neighbor nearby than a brother far away.

—*Proverbs 27:10 (NKJV)*

Dear children, let's not merely say that we love each other; let us show the truth by our actions.

—*1 John 3:18 (NLT)*

We don't need to write to you about having love for your brothers and sisters in Christ. God has already taught you to love each other. And truly you do love the brothers and sisters in all of Macedonia. Brothers and sisters, now we encourage you to love them more and more.

—*1 Thessalonians 4:9–10 (ERV)*

A friend loves at all times, and a brother is born for adversity.

—*Proverbs 17:17 (NKJV)*

Since God chose you to be the holy people he loves, you must clothe yourselves with tenderhearted mercy, kindness, humility, gentleness, and patience. Make allowance for each other's faults, and forgive anyone who offends you. Remember, the Lord forgave you, so you must forgive others. Above all, clothe yourselves with love, which binds us all together in perfect harmony.

—Colossians 3:12–14 (NLT)

And let us consider how we may spur one another on toward love and good deeds.

—Hebrews 10:24 (NIV)

Some friends are fun to be with. But a close friend can be even better than a brother.

—Proverbs 18:24 (ERV)

And do everything with love.
—*1 Corinthians 16:14 (NLT)*

But I say to you, love your enemies,
bless those who curse you, do good to
those who hate you, and pray for those
who spitefully use you and persecute
you, that you may be sons of your
Father in heaven; for He makes His
sun rise on the evil and on the good,
and sends rain on the just and on the
unjust.
—*Matthew 5:44–45 (NKJV)*

Do not gloat when your enemy falls;
when he stumbles, do not let your heart
rejoice.
—*Proverbs 24:17 (NIV)*

God has chosen you and made you his holy people. He loves you. So always do these things: Show mercy to people; be kind, humble, gentle, and patient.
—*Colossians 3:12 (ERV)*

He who covers a transgression seeks love, but he who repeats a matter separates friends.
—*Proverbs 17:9 (NKJV)*

If someone does wrong to you, don't pay him back by doing wrong to him. Try to do the things that all people think are good. Do the best you can to live in peace with all people.
—*Romans 12:17–18 (ERV)*

Be completely humble and gentle; be patient, bearing with one another in love. Make every effort to keep the unity of the Spirit through the bond of peace.
—*Ephesians 4:2–3 (NIV)*

Aim for perfection, listen to my appeal, be of one mind, live in peace. And the God of love and peace will be with you.
—*2 Corinthians 13:11 (NIV)*

And above all things have fervent love for one another, for "love will cover a multitude of sins." Be hospitable to one another without grumbling. As each one has received a gift, minister it to one another, as good stewards of the manifold grace of God.
—*1 Peter 4:8–10 (NKJV)*

When you are praying, and you remember that you are angry with another person about something, then forgive that person. Forgive them so that your Father in heaven will also forgive your sins.
—*Mark 11:25 (ERV)*

Make sure that nobody pays back wrong for wrong, but always try to be kind to each other and to everyone else.
—*1 Thessalonians 5:15 (NIV)*

But to you who are willing to listen, I say, love your enemies! Do good to those who hate you. Bless those who curse you. Pray for those who hurt you. . . . Give to anyone who asks; and when things are taken away from you, don't try to get them back. Do to others as you would like them to do to you.
—*Luke 6:27–28, 30–31 (NLT)*

By this all will know that you are My disciples, if you have love for one another.
—*John 13:35 (NKJV)*

Do to others as you would have them do to you.
—*Luke 6:31 (NIV)*

Do not take revenge, my friends, but leave room for God's wrath, for it is written: "It is mine to avenge; I will repay," says the Lord. On the contrary: "If your enemy is hungry, feed him; if he is thirsty, give him something to drink. In doing this, you will heap burning coals on his head." Do not be overcome by evil, but overcome evil with good.

—Romans 12:19–21 (NIV)

Finally, all of you be of one mind, having compassion for one another; love as brothers, be tenderhearted, be courteous; not returning evil for evil or reviling for reviling, but on the contrary blessing, knowing that you were called to this, that you may inherit a blessing.

—1 Peter 3:8–9 (NKJV)

Make allowance for each other's faults, and forgive anyone who offends you. Remember, the Lord forgave you, so you must forgive others. Above all, clothe yourselves with love, which binds us all together in perfect harmony.

—*Colossians 3:13–14 (NLT)*

But I tell you not to resist an evil person. But whoever slaps you on your right cheek, turn the other to him also. If anyone wants to sue you and take away your tunic, let him have your cloak also. And whoever compels you to go one mile, go with him two. Give to him who asks you, and from him who wants to borrow from you do not turn away.

—*Matthew 5:39–42 (NKJV)*

Hatred stirs up quarrels, but love makes up for all offenses.

—*Proverbs 10:12 (NLT)*

Sensible people control their temper; they earn respect by overlooking wrongs.
—*Proverbs 19:11 (NLT)*

So let us try as hard as we can to do the things that make peace. And let us try to do the things that will help each other.
—*Romans 14:19 (ERV)*

Loving MEANS FORGIVING

Judge not, and you shall not be judged. Condemn not, and you shall not be condemned. Forgive, and you will be forgiven.

—*Luke 6:37 (NKJV)*

Then Peter came to Him and said, "Lord, how often shall my brother sin against me, and I forgive him? Up to seven times?" Jesus said to him, "I do not say to you, up to seven times, but up to seventy times seven."

—*Matthew 18:21–22 (NKJV)*

And when you stand praying, if you hold anything against anyone, forgive him, so that your Father in heaven may forgive you your sins.

—*Mark 11:25 (NIV)*

God has chosen you and made you his holy people. He loves you. So always do these things: Show mercy to people; be kind, humble, gentle, and patient. Don't be angry with each other, but forgive each other. If another person does something wrong against you, then forgive that person. Forgive other people because the Lord forgave you. Do all these things; but most important, love each other. Love is the thing that holds you all together in perfect unity.

—*Colossians 3:12–14 (ERV)*

And do not grieve the Holy Spirit of God, with whom you were sealed for the day of redemption. . . . Be kind and compassionate to one another, forgiving each other, just as in Christ God forgave you.

—*Ephesians 4:30, 32 (NIV)*

A person says, "I am in the light." But if that person hates his brother or sister in Christ, then he is still in the darkness (sin). The person that loves his brothers and sisters lives in the light, and there is nothing in that person that will make him do wrong.

—*1 John 2:9–10 (ERV)*

When you forgive this man, I forgive him, too. And when I forgive whatever needs to be forgiven, I do so with Christ's authority for your benefit.

—*2 Corinthians 2:10 (NLT)*

And forgive us our debts, as we forgive our debtors. . . . For if you forgive men their trespasses, your heavenly Father will also forgive you. But if you do not forgive men their trespasses, neither will your Father forgive your trespasses.

—*Matthew 6:12, 14–15 (NKJV)*

So watch yourselves! If another believer sins, rebuke that person; then if there is repentance, forgive. Even if that person wrongs you seven times a day and each time turns again and asks forgiveness, you must forgive.

—*Luke 17:3–4 (NLT)*

Loving MEANS ENCOURAGING

But encourage each other every day.
Do this while it is "today." Help each
other so that none of you will become
hardened because of sin and the way
sin fools people.

—*Hebrews 3:13 (ERV)*

Therefore encourage one another and
build each other up, just as in fact you
are doing.

—*1 Thessalonians 5:11 (NIV)*

My dear brothers and sisters, always
be more willing to listen than to speak.
Don't become angry easily.

—*James 1:19 (ERV)*

Do you have the gift of speaking? Then speak as though God himself were speaking through you. Do you have the gift of helping others? Do it with all the strength and energy that God supplies. Then everything you do will bring glory to God through Jesus Christ. All glory and power to him forever and ever! Amen.

—*1 Peter 4:11 (NLT)*

My little children, let us not love in word or in tongue, but in deed and in truth.

—*1 John 3:18 (NKJV)*

Be of the same mind toward one another. Do not set your mind on high things, but associate with the humble. Do not be wise in your own opinion.

—*Romans 12:16 (NKJV)*

In his grace, God has given us different gifts for doing certain things well. So if God has given you the ability to prophesy, speak out with as much faith as God has given you. If your gift is serving others, serve them well. If you are a teacher, teach well. If your gift is to encourage others, be encouraging. If it is giving, give generously. If God has given you leadership ability, take the responsibility seriously. And if you have a gift for showing kindness to others, do it gladly.

—Romans 12:6–8 (NLT)

Be completely humble and gentle; be patient, bearing with one another in love.

—Ephesians 4:2 (NIV)

So let's stop condemning each other. Decide instead to live in such a way that you will not cause another believer to stumble and fall.

—Romans 14:13 (NLT)

Reckless words pierce like a sword, but the tongue of the wise brings healing.

—Proverbs 12:18 (NIV)

Speaking to one another in psalms and hymns and spiritual songs, singing and making melody in your heart to the Lord.

—Ephesians 5:19 (NKJV)

We pray that the Lord Jesus Christ himself and God our Father will comfort you and strengthen you in every good thing you do and say. God loved us. Through his grace (kindness) he gave us a good hope and comfort that continues forever.

—2 Thessalonians 2:16–17 (ERV)

Is there any way in Christ that I can ask you to do something? Does your love make you want to comfort me? Do we share together in the Spirit? Do you have mercy and kindness? If you have these things, then I ask you to do something for me. This will make me very happy. I ask that all your minds be joined together by believing the same things. Be joined together in your love for each other. Live together by agreeing with each other and having the same goals. When you do things, don't let selfishness or pride be your guide. Be humble and give more honor to other people than to yourselves. Don't be interested only in your own life, but be interested in the lives of other people, too.

—*Philippians 2:1–4 (ERV)*

Cheerfully share your home with those who need a meal or a place to stay.
—*1 Peter 4:9 (NLT)*

Finally, all of you be of one mind, having compassion for one another; love as brothers, be tenderhearted, be courteous.
—*1 Peter 3:8 (NKJV)*

Christ accepted you. So you should accept each other. This will bring glory to God.
—*Romans 15:7 (ERV)*

Loving
MEANS HELPING YOUR NEIGHBOR

Share with God's people that need help.
Look for people that need help, and
welcome those people into your homes.
 —*Romans 12:13 (ERV)*

This is how we know what love is:
Jesus Christ laid down his life for us.
And we ought to lay down our lives for
our brothers. If anyone has material
possessions and sees his brother in
need but has no pity on him, how
can the love of God be in him? Dear
children, let us not love with words or
tongue but with actions and in truth.
 —*1 John 3:16–18 (NIV)*

Owe no one anything except to love one another, for he who loves another has fulfilled the law. For the commandments, "You shall not commit adultery," "You shall not murder," "You shall not steal," "You shall not bear false witness," "You shall not covet," and if there is any other commandment, are all summed up in this saying, namely, "You shall love your neighbor as yourself." Love does no harm to a neighbor; therefore love is the fulfillment of the law.

—*Romans 13:8–10 (NKJV)*

Most important, love each other deeply. Love hides many, many sins. Share your homes with each other without complaining.

—*1 Peter 4:8–9 (ERV)*

For all the law is fulfilled in one word, even in this: "You shall love your neighbor as yourself."
—*Galatians 5:14 (NKJV)*

Jesus replied: "'Love the Lord your God with all your heart and with all your soul and with all your mind.' This is the first and greatest commandment. And the second is like it: 'Love your neighbor as yourself.' All the Law and the Prophets hang on these two commandments."
—*Matthew 22:37–40 (NIV)*

If you can help your neighbor now, don't say, "Come back tomorrow, and then I'll help you."
—*Proverbs 3:28 (NLT)*

So in everything, do to others what you would have them do to you, for this sums up the Law and the Prophets.
—*Matthew 7:12 (NIV)*

You have heard that it was said, "Love your neighbor and hate your enemy." But I tell you, love your enemies. Pray for those people that do bad things to you. If you do this, then you will be true sons of your Father in heaven. Your Father lets the sun rise for the good people and the bad people. Your Father sends rain to people that do good and to people that do wrong. If you love only the people that love you, then you will get no reward. Even the tax collectors do that. And if you are nice only to your friends, then you are no better than other people. Even the people without God are nice to their friends.

—*Matthew 5:43–47 (ERV)*

He who says he is in the light, and hates his brother, is in darkness until now.

—*1 John 2:9 (NKJV)*

The kind of religion (worship) that God accepts is this: caring for orphans or widows who need help, and keeping yourself free from the world's evil influence. This is the kind of religion (worship) that God accepts as pure and good.

—*James 1:27 (ERV)*

What does it profit, my brethren, if someone says he has faith but does not have works? Can faith save him? If a brother or sister is naked and destitute of daily food, and one of you says to them, "Depart in peace, be warmed and filled," but you do not give them the things which are needed for the body, what does it profit? Thus also faith by itself, if it does not have works, is dead.

—*James 2:14–17 (NKJV)*

One day an expert in religious law stood up to test Jesus by asking him this question: "Teacher, what should I do to inherit eternal life?"

Jesus replied, "What does the law of Moses say? How do you read it?"

The man answered, "'You must love the LORD your God with all your heart, all your soul, all your strength, and all your mind.' And, 'Love your neighbor as yourself.'"

"Right!" Jesus told him. "Do this and you will live!"

—*Luke 10:25–28 (NLT)*

Don't make plans to hurt your neighbor. You live near each other for your own safety!

—*Proverbs 3:29 (ERV)*

But love your enemies, do good to them, and lend to them without expecting to get anything back. Then your reward will be great, and you will be sons of the Most High, because he is kind to the ungrateful and wicked. Be merciful, just as your Father is merciful.

—*Luke 6:35–36 (NIV)*